# ENGLISH
## FOR EVERYONE
# JUNIOR
# ENGLISH DICTIONARY

**FREE AUDIO**
website and app

www.dkefe.com/junior/us

# ENGLISH FOR EVERYONE
## JUNIOR
## ENGLISH DICTIONARY

**FREE AUDIO**
website and app

 www.dkefe.com/junior/us

For the curious

**DK LONDON**
**Project Editor** Sophie Adam
**Project Art Editor** Annabel Schick
**Illustrator** Gus Scott
**Managing Editor** Christine Stroyan
**Managing Art Editor** Anna Hall
**Production Editor** George Nimmo
**Production Controller** Samantha Cross
**Senior Jacket Designer** Surabhi Wadhwa-Gandhi
**Jacket Design Development Manager** Sophia MTT
**Publisher** Andrew Macintyre
**Art Director** Karen Self
**Publishing Director** Jonathan Metcalf

**DK DELHI**
**Jacket Designer** Juhi Sheth
**DTP Designer** Rakesh Kumar
**Senior Jackets Editorial Coordinator** Priyanka Sharma

This American Boxset Edition, 2024
First American Edition, 2021
Published in the United States by DK Publishing
a Division of Penguin Random House LLC
1745 Broadway, 20th Floor, New York, NY 10019

Copyright © 2021, 2024 Dorling Kindersley Limited
24 25 26 27 10 9 8 7 6 5 4 3 2 1
001–340278–Jun/2024

All rights reserved.
Without limiting the rights under the copyright reserved above, no part of this publication may be reproduced, stored in or introduced into a retrieval system, or transmitted, in any form, or by any means (electronic, mechanical, photocopying, recording, or otherwise), without the prior written permission of the copyright owner. Published in Great Britain by Dorling Kindersley Limited

A catalog record for this book
is available from the Library of Congress.
Boxset ISBN 978-0-5938-4226-3
Book ISBN 978-0-7440-4573-4

DK books are available at special discounts when purchased in bulk for sales promotions, premiums, fund-raising, or educational use. For details, contact: DK Publishing Special Markets, 1745 Broadway, 20th Floor, New York, NY 10019
SpecialSales@dk.com

Printed and bound in China

www.dk.com

This book was made with Forest Stewardship Council™ certified paper – one small step in DK's commitment to a sustainable future. Learn more at www.dk.com/uk/information/sustainability

# Contents

About this book ......... 6
The alphabet ......... 8
A ......... 10
B ......... 14
C ......... 24
D ......... 34
E ......... 38
F ......... 40
G ......... 46
H ......... 50
I ......... 56
J ......... 58
K ......... 60
L ......... 62
M ......... 66
N ......... 70

# Meet the characters

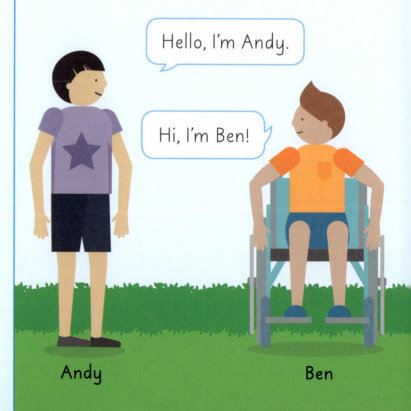

Hello, I'm Andy.

Hi, I'm Ben!

Andy                Ben

| | |
|---|---|
| O | 72 |
| P | 74 |
| Q | 83 |
| R | 84 |
| S | 88 |
| T | 104 |
| U | 112 |
| V | 112 |

| | |
|---|---|
| W | 114 |
| X | 118 |
| Y | 118 |
| Z | 119 |
| Numbers | 120 |
| In the classroom | 121 |
| Time | 122 |
| Prepositions | 123 |

| | |
|---|---|
| Directions | 123 |
| Positions | 123 |
| Useful phrases | 124 |
| Feelings | 125 |
| Opposites | 126 |
| Word list | 130 |

Maria   Max   Sara   Sofia

# About this book

*English for Everyone Junior: English Dictionary* is an A–Z vocabulary book for children that introduces more than 1,000 English words through colorful illustrations. You can access audio recordings for all the words, phrases, and songs featured in this book on the accompanying website and app.

The letter bar helps you remember the order of the alphabet and find your place in the book.

Read the words on the page, listen to the audio, and repeat each new word out loud.

Vocabulary sets taught inside boxes are grouped by subject, rather than alphetically.

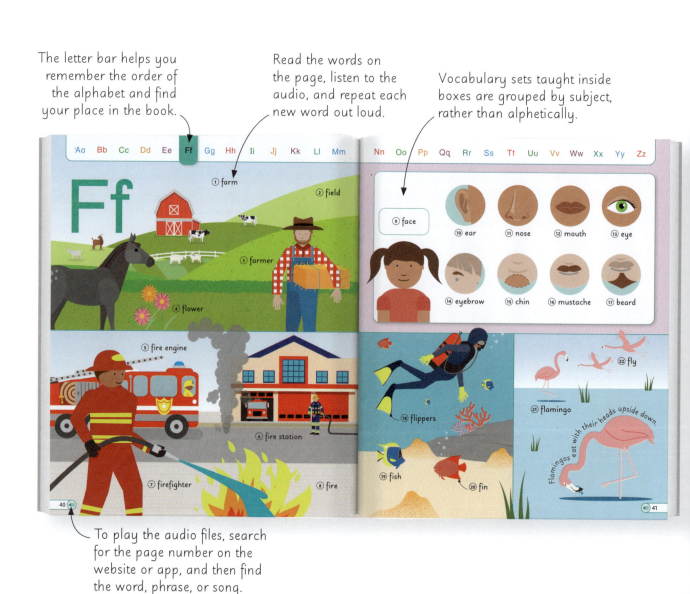

To play the audio files, search for the page number on the website or app, and then find the word, phrase, or song.

## Audio

Pronunciation is an important aspect of learning a new language. Access the free audio material for this book on the **English for Everyone Junior** website and app. Visit **www.dkefe.com/junior/us** or download the **DK English for Everyone Junior** app from the App Store or Google Play.

**FREE AUDIO**
website and app

**www.dkefe.com/junior/us**

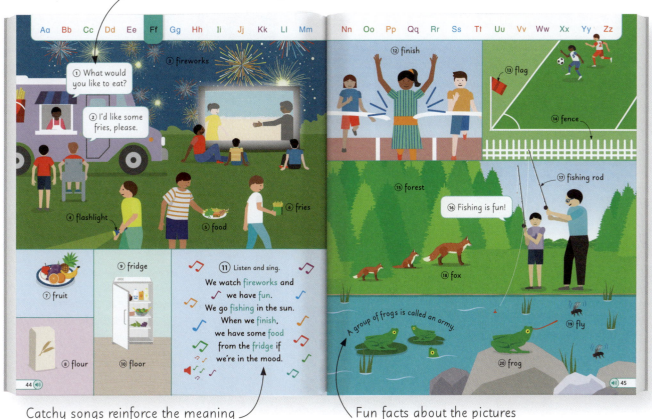

Speech bubbles feature useful phrases and additional vocabulary.

Catchy songs reinforce the meaning of new words. Listen and sing along to develop your pronunciation.

Fun facts about the pictures help you build new vocabulary.

# The alphabet

The English alphabet has 26 letters. Use capital letters for the first letter of a sentence, the names of people or places, the days of the week, and the months of the year. Use lowercase letters the rest of the time. Trace the letters with your finger, starting at the white dot. Listen to the audio and repeat each letter, then listen to the song and sing along.

Mm Nn Oo
Pp Qq Rr
Ss Tt Uu
Vv Ww Xx
Yy Zz

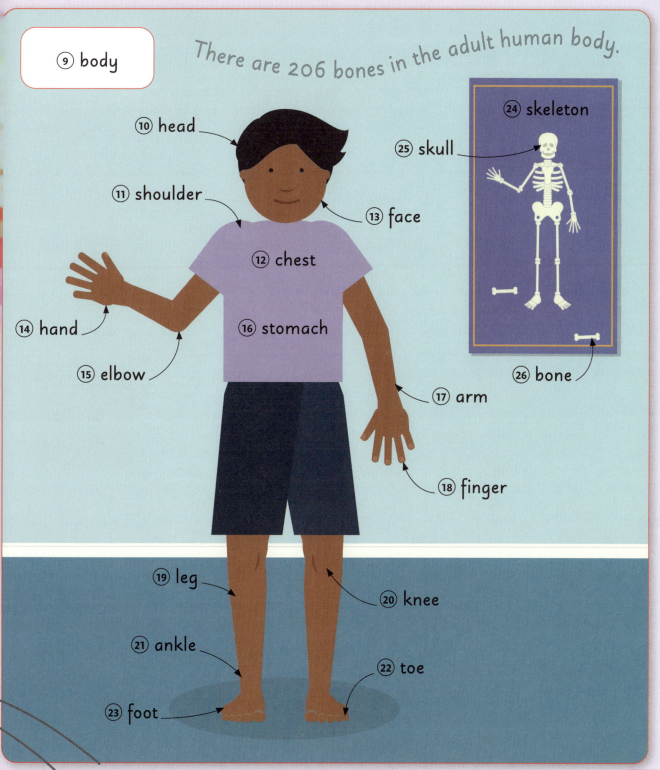

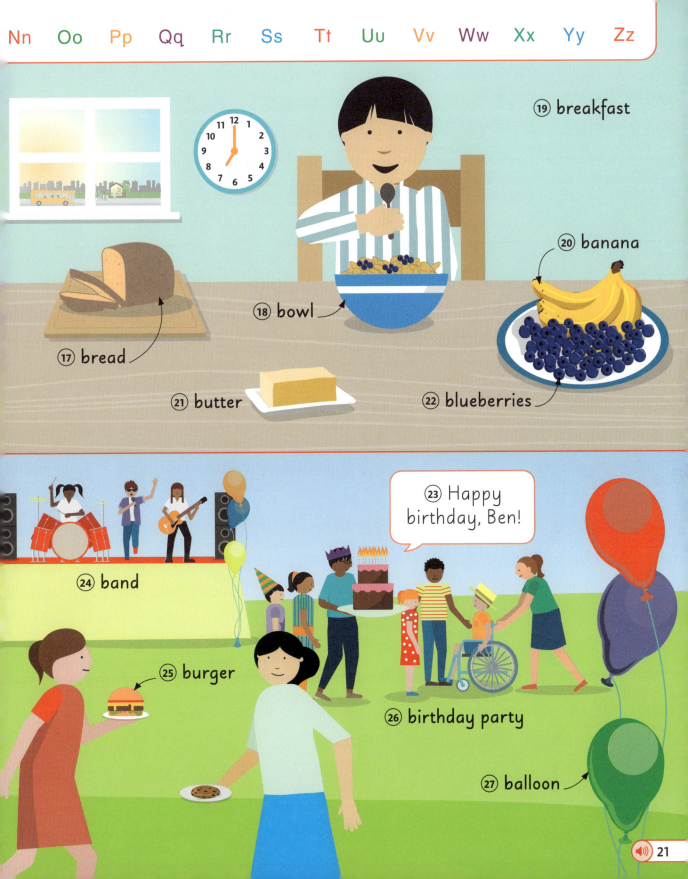

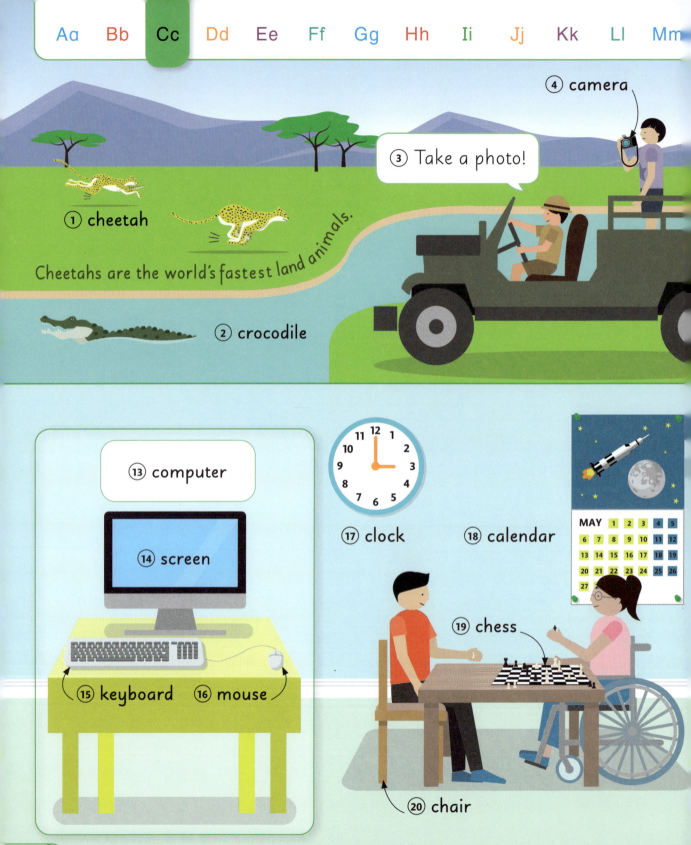

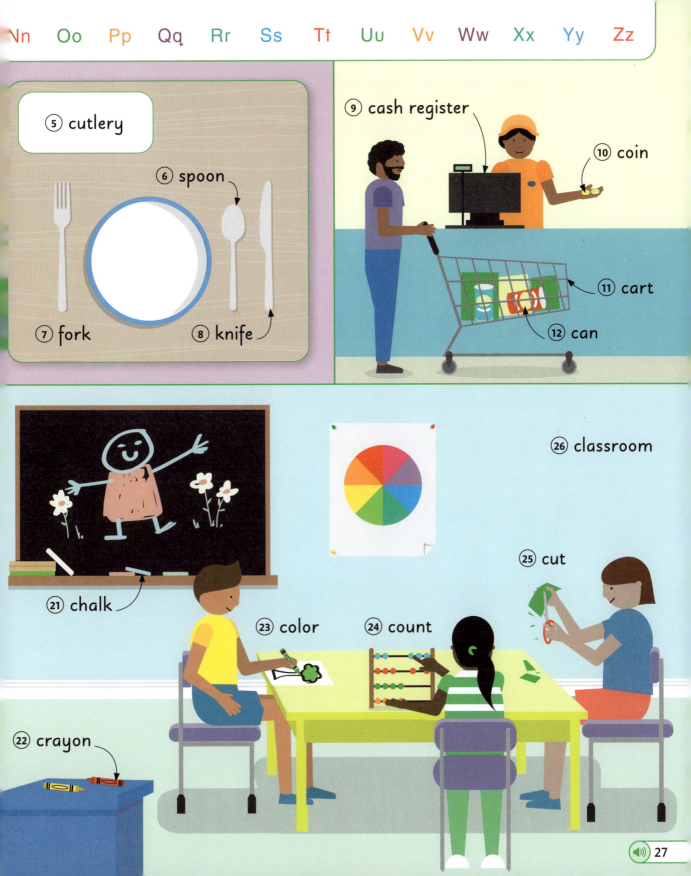

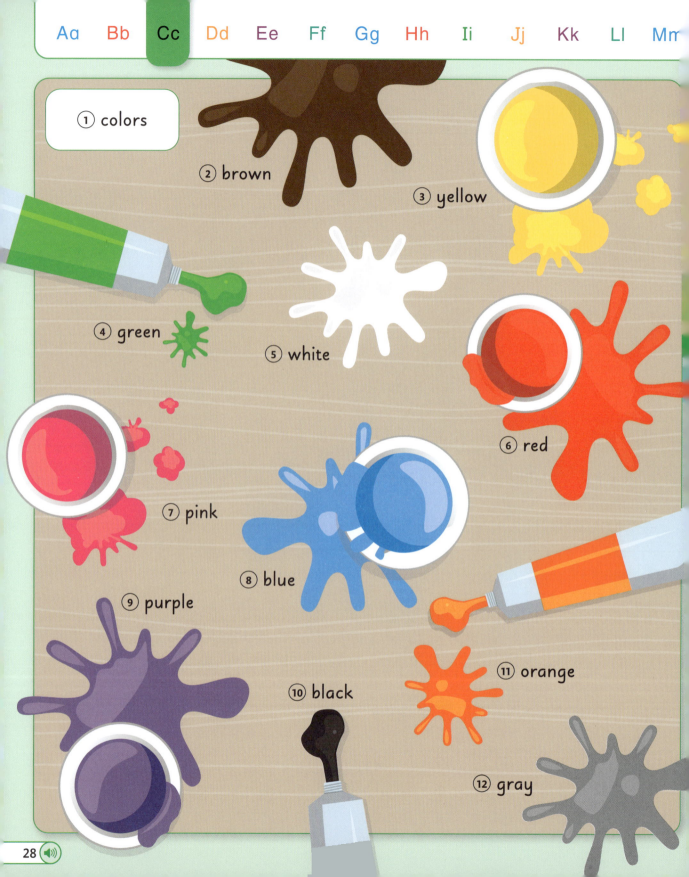

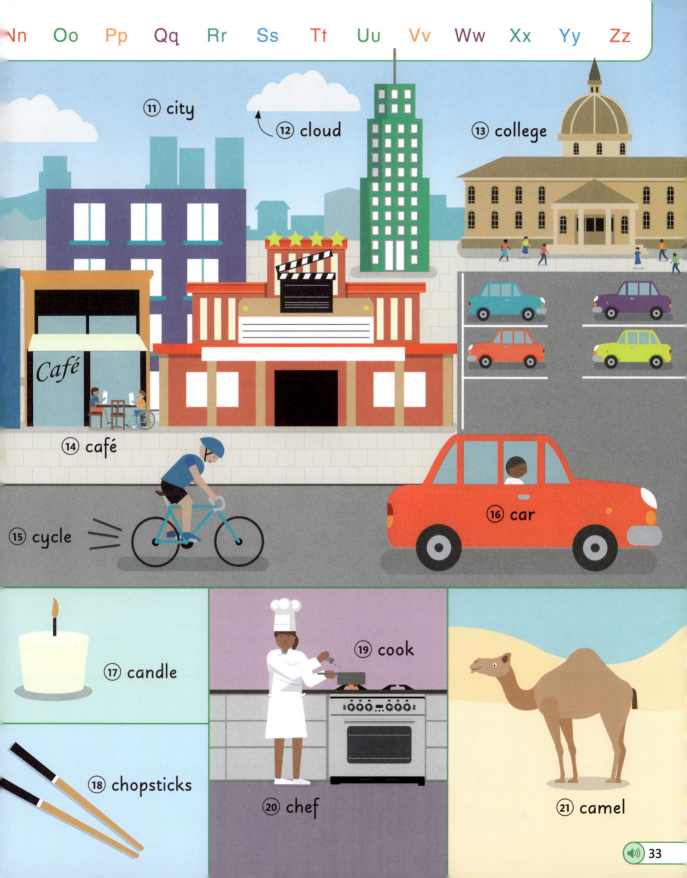

Nn  Oo  Pp  Qq  Rr  Ss  Tt  Uu  Vv  Ww  Xx  Yy  Zz

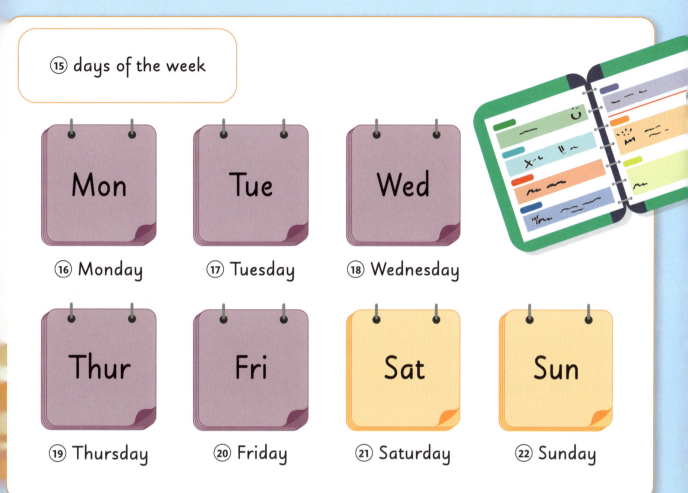

⑮ days of the week

⑯ Monday
⑰ Tuesday
⑱ Wednesday
⑲ Thursday
⑳ Friday
㉑ Saturday
㉒ Sunday

㉓ Listen and sing.

On Monday, I dreamed about dragons.
On Tuesday, I played my drum.
On Wednesday, I drew a picture of a dinosaur in the sun.
On Thursday, I saw the doctor, and I took my doll with me.
On Friday, I went to the beach, and there were dolphins in the sea.

37

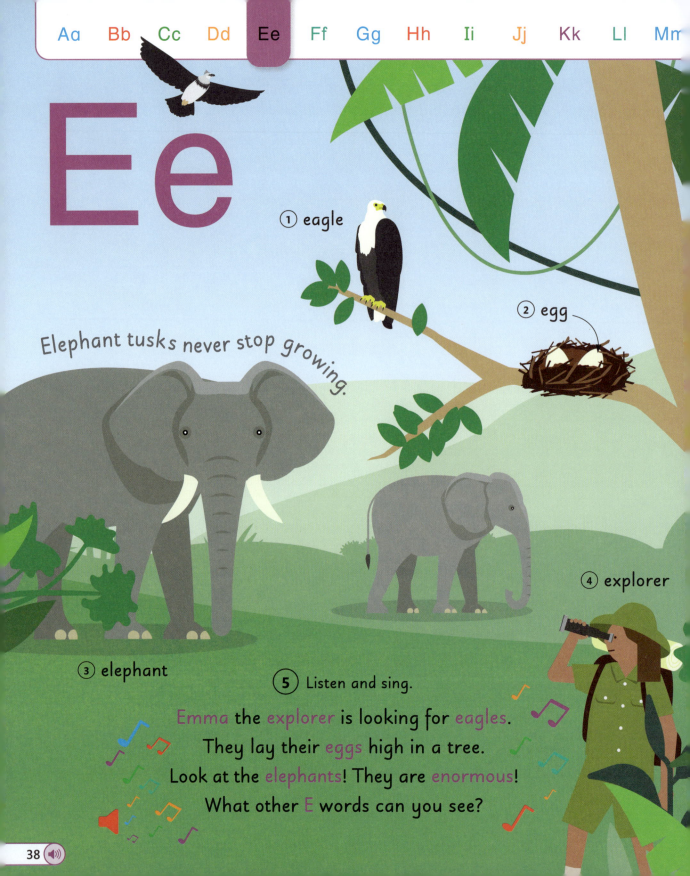

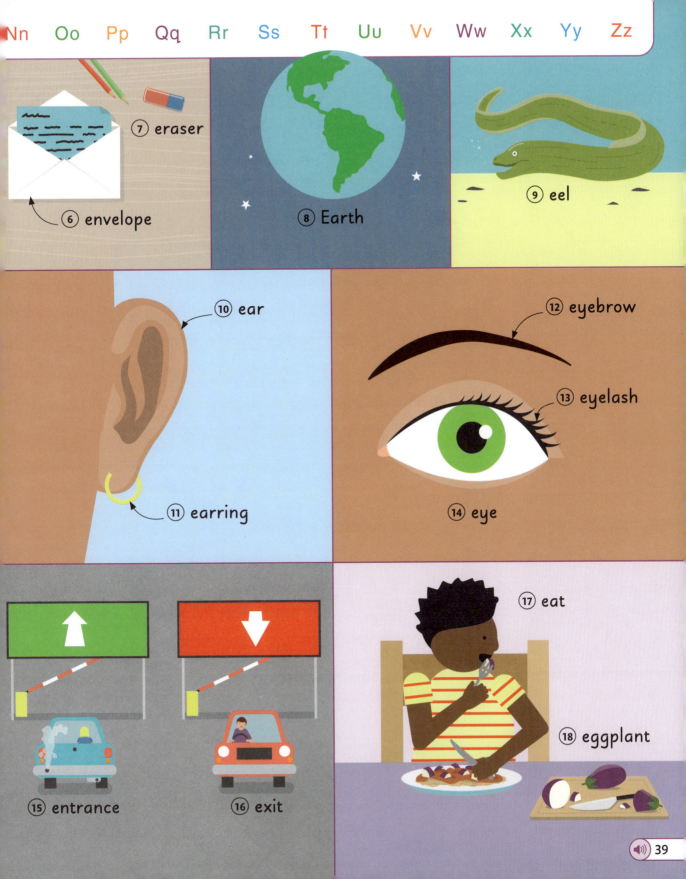

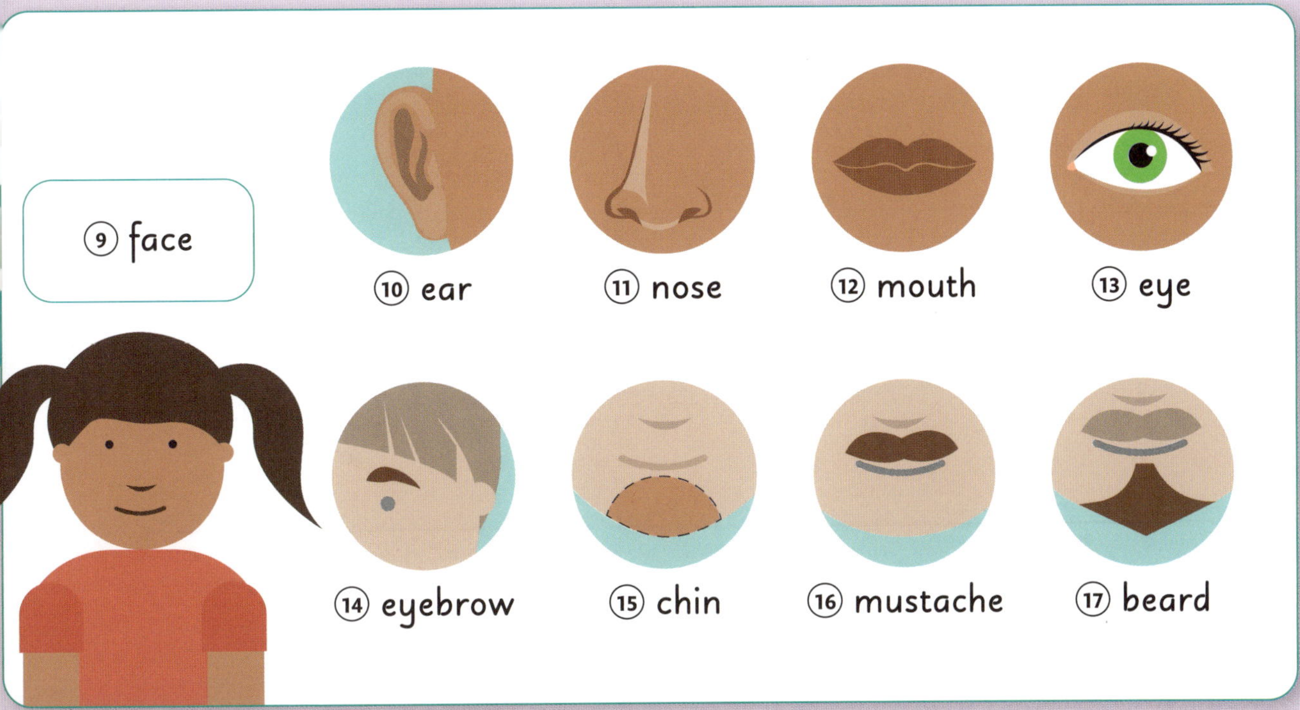

Nn　Oo　Pp　Qq　Rr　Ss　Tt　Uu　Vv　Ww　Xx　Yy　Zz

⑨ face
⑩ ear
⑪ nose
⑫ mouth
⑬ eye
⑭ eyebrow
⑮ chin
⑯ mustache
⑰ beard

⑱ flippers
⑲ fish
⑳ fin
㉑ flamingo 
㉒ fly

Flamingos eat with their heads upside down.

41

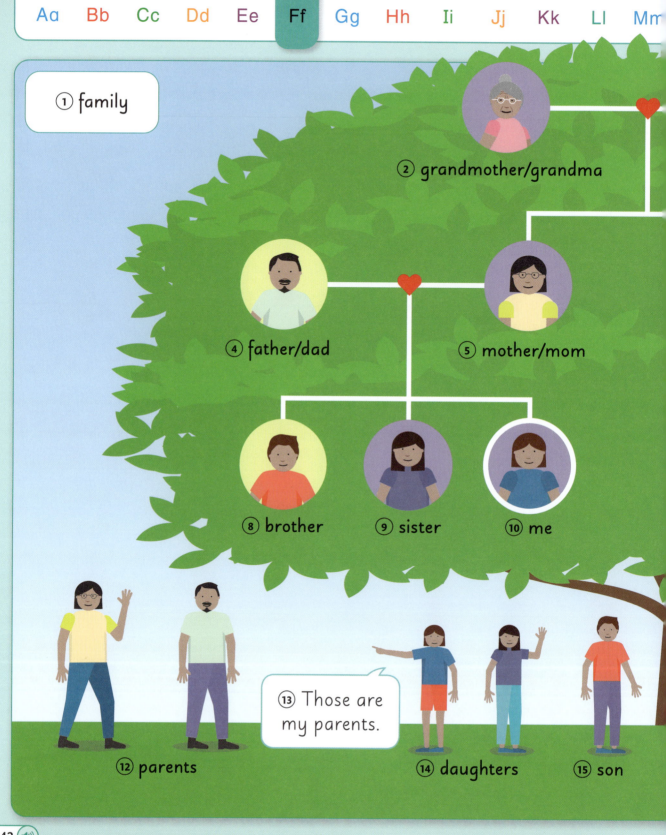

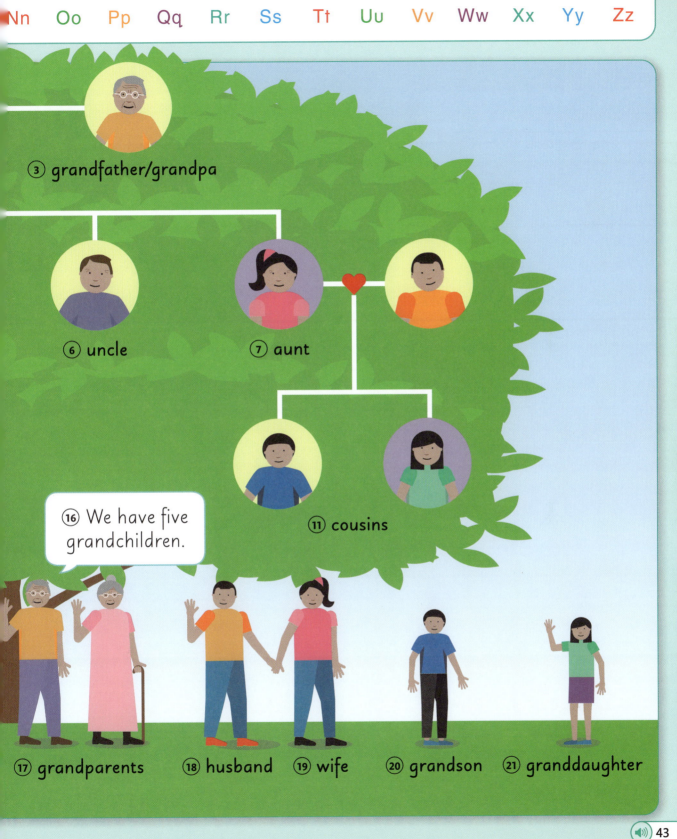

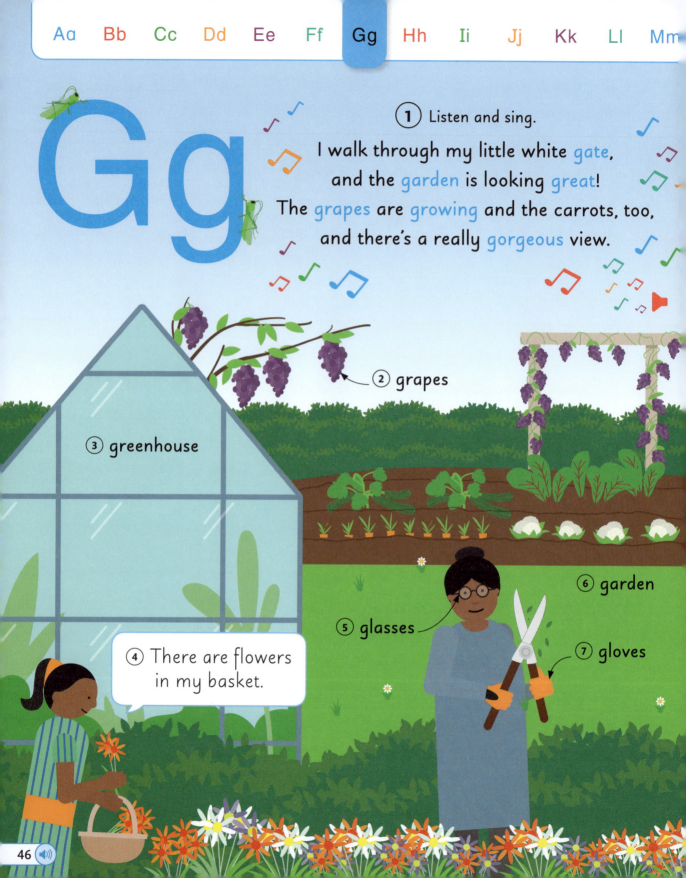

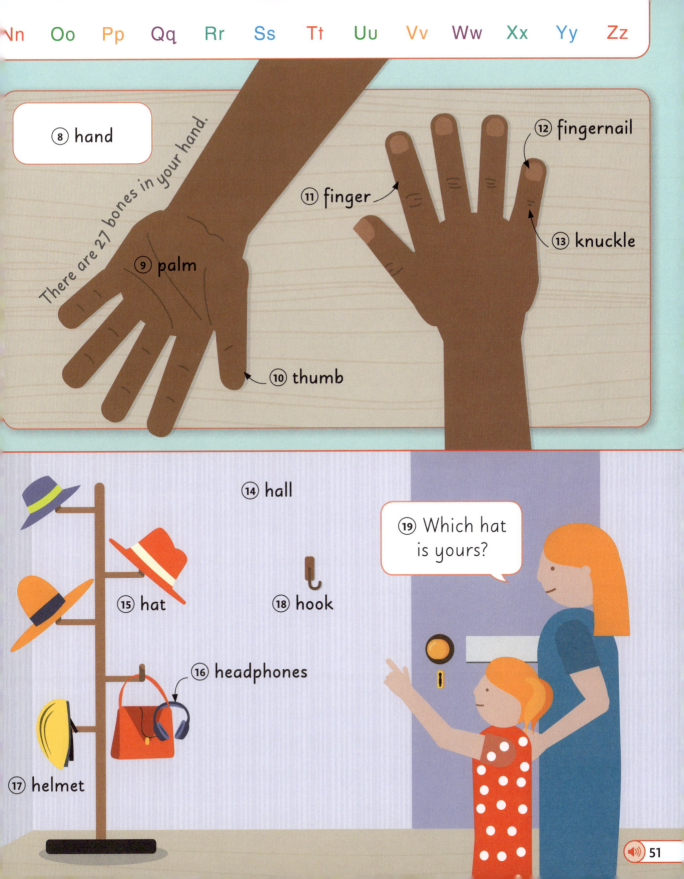

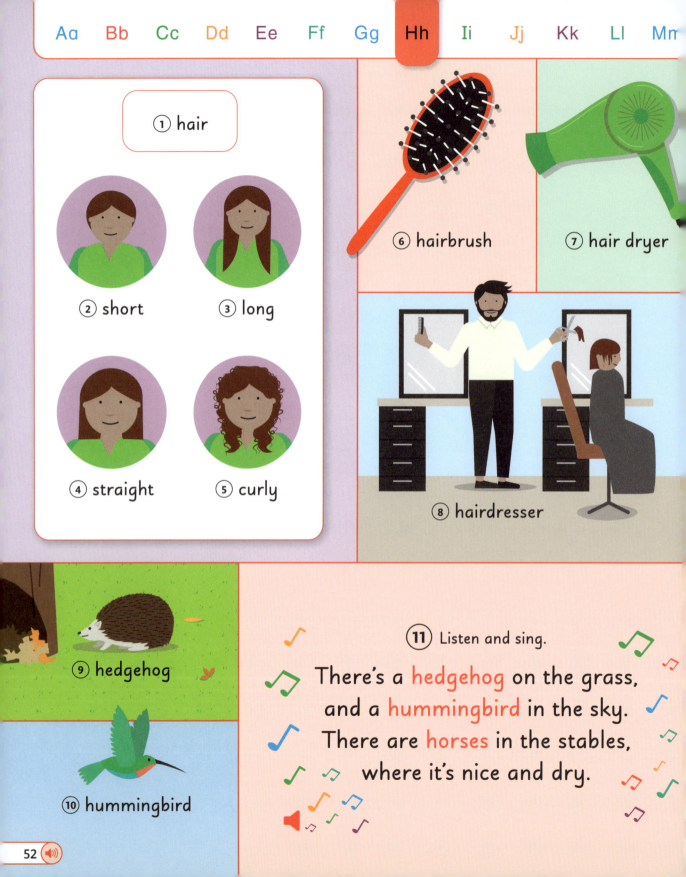

Nn　Oo　Pp　Qq　Rr　Ss　Tt　Uu　Vv　Ww　Xx　Yy　Zz

 ⑩ cold

 ⑪ sick

 ⑫ cough

 ⑬ stomachache

 ⑭ earache

 ⑮ headache

 ⑯ sore

 ⑰ nauseated

 ⑱ sneeze

55

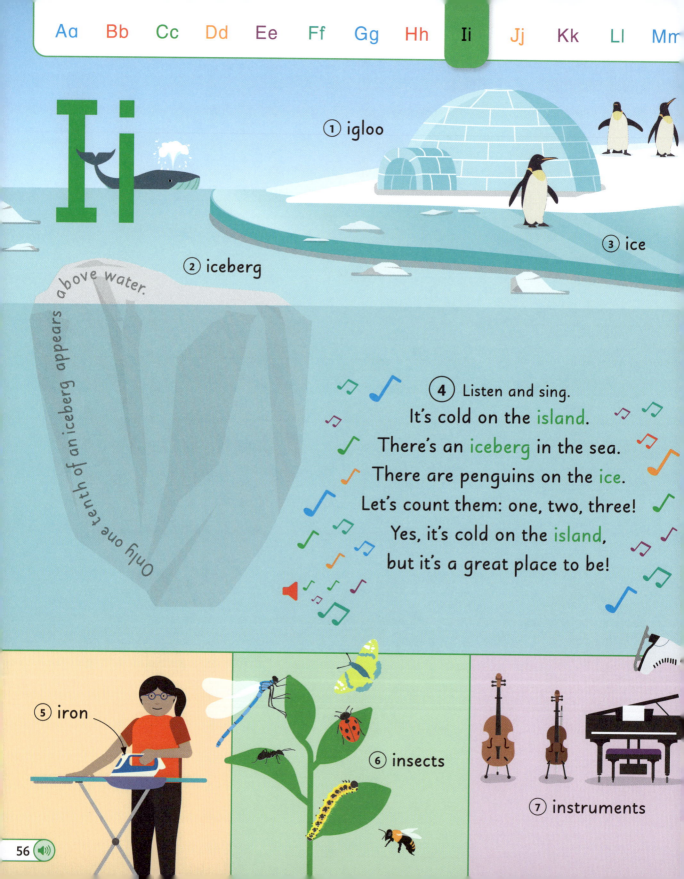

| Aa | Bb | Cc | Dd | Ee | Ff | Gg | Hh | Ii | Jj | **Kk** | Ll | Mm |

# Kk

Baby kangaroos are called joeys.

① kangaroo
② koala

③ Listen and sing.

The king keeps his keys in his pocket.
The cat keeps her kitten by her side.
Kangaroos keep their joeys in a pouch,
so the babies are comfortable inside.

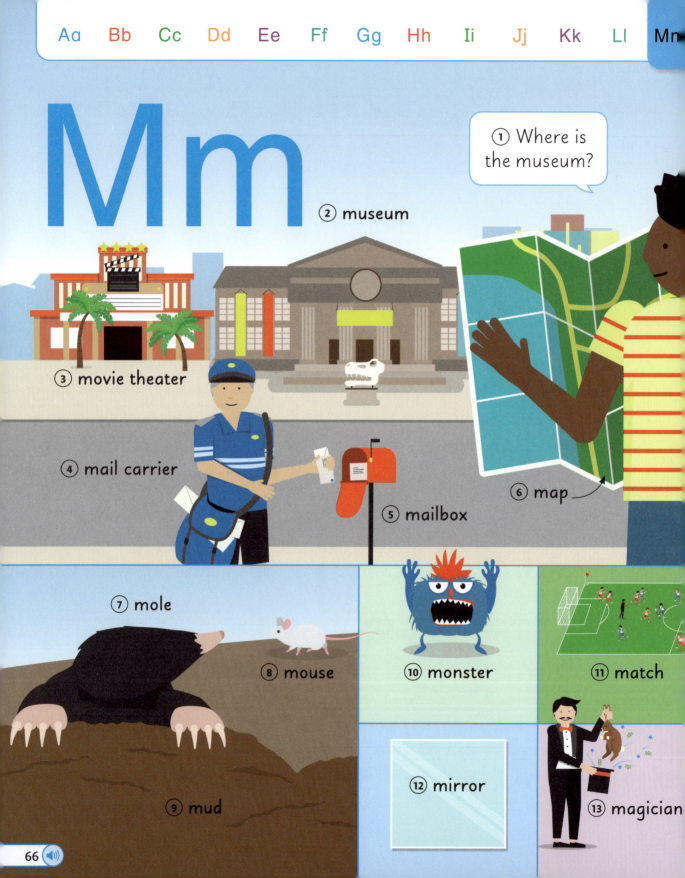

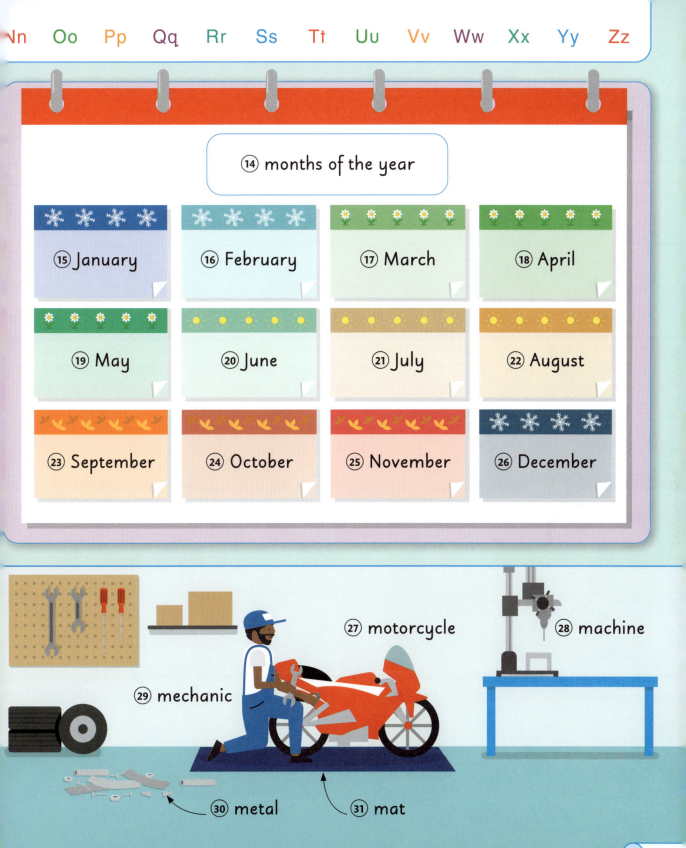

Nn  Oo  Pp  Qq  Rr  Ss  Tt  Uu  Vv  Ww  Xx  Yy  Zz

⑫ numbers

**1** ⑬ one
**2** ⑭ two
**3** ⑮ three
**4** ⑯ four
**5** ⑰ five

**6** ⑱ six
**7** ⑲ seven
**8** ⑳ eight
**9** ㉑ nine
**10** ㉒ ten

**11** ㉓ eleven
**12** ㉔ twelve
**13** ㉕ thirteen
**14** ㉖ fourteen
**15** ㉗ fifteen

**16** ㉘ sixteen
**17** ㉙ seventeen
**18** ㉚ eighteen
**19** ㉛ nineteen
**20** ㉜ twenty

71

Aa  Bb  Cc  Dd  Ee  Ff  Gg  Hh  Ii  Jj  Kk  Ll  Mm

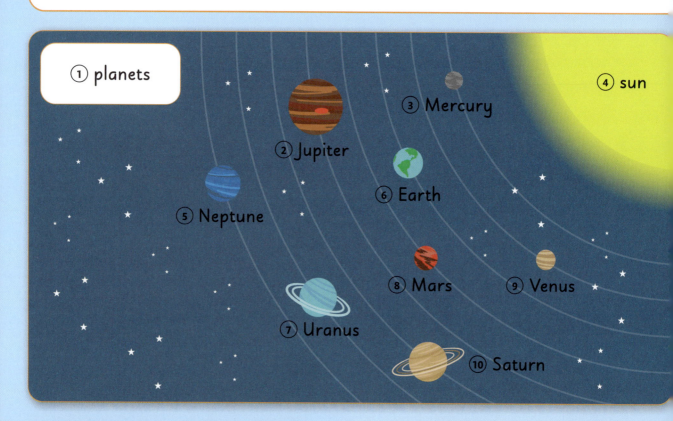

① planets
② Jupiter
③ Mercury
④ sun
⑤ Neptune
⑥ Earth
⑦ Uranus
⑧ Mars
⑨ Venus
⑩ Saturn

⑪ palace
⑫ peacock

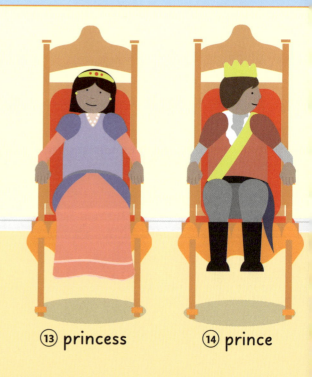

⑬ princess
⑭ prince

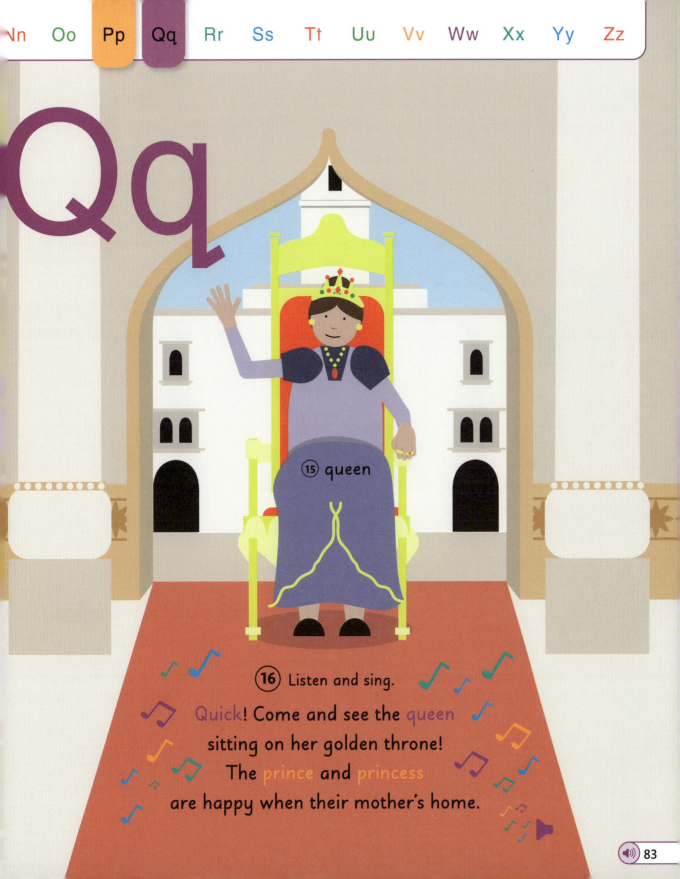

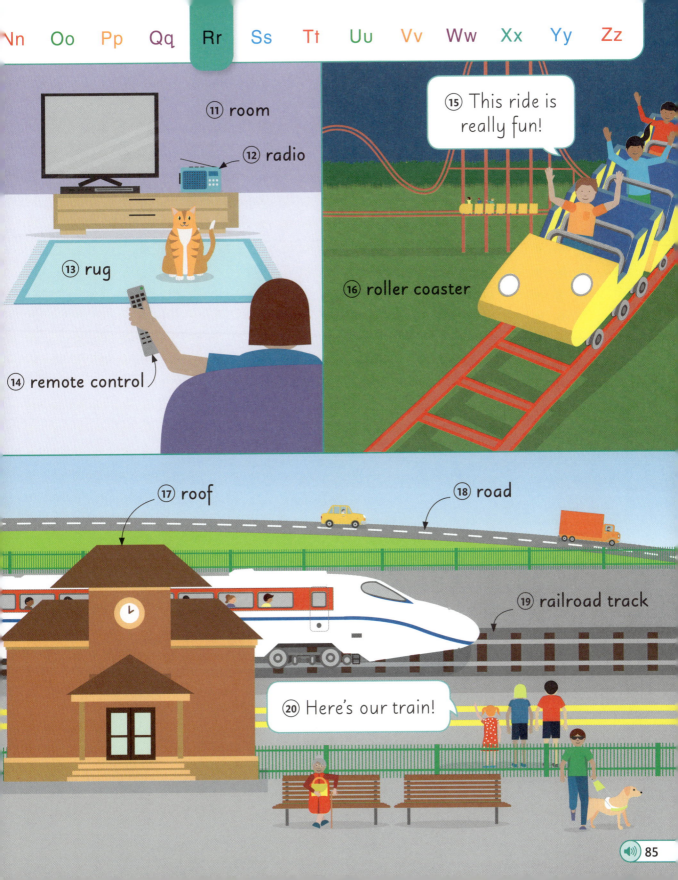

Nn  Oo  Pp  Qq  Rr  **Ss**  Tt  Uu  Vv  Ww  Xx  Yy  Zz

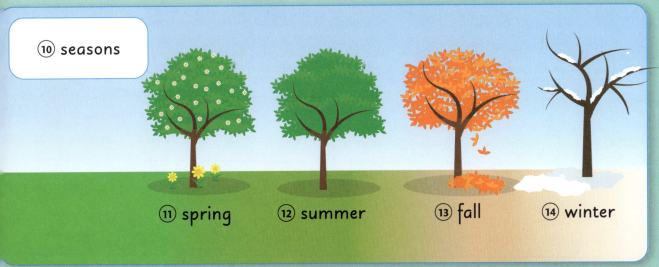

⑩ seasons
⑪ spring
⑫ summer
⑬ fall
⑭ winter

⑮ salad
⑯ spinach
⑰ soup
⑱ spoon
⑲ sandwich

97

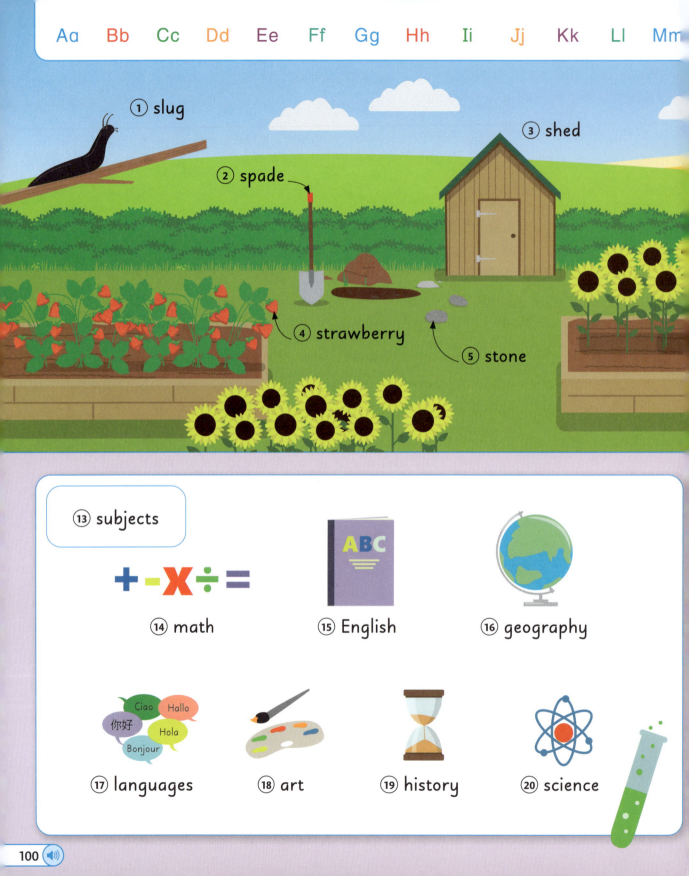

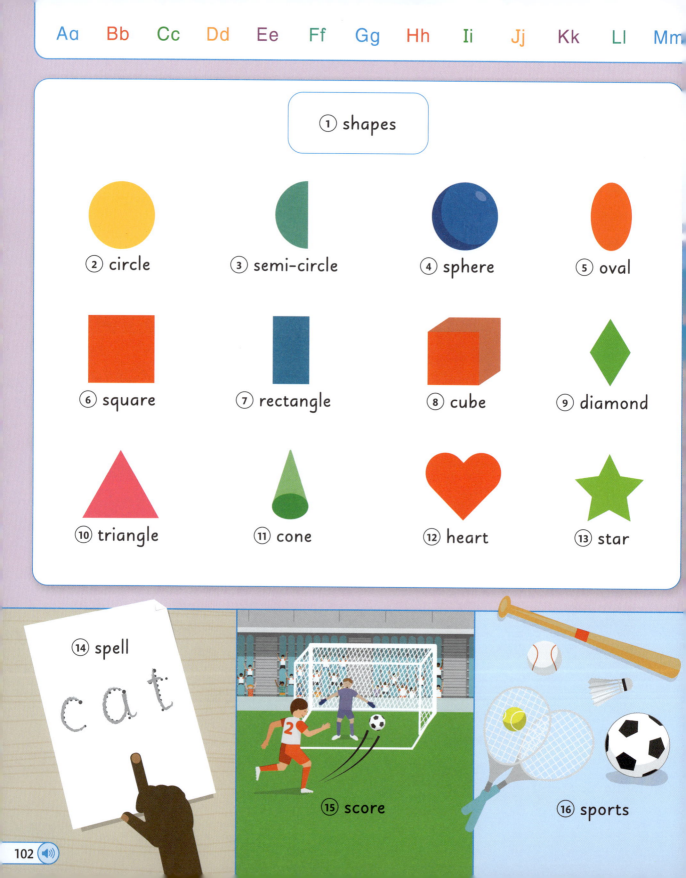

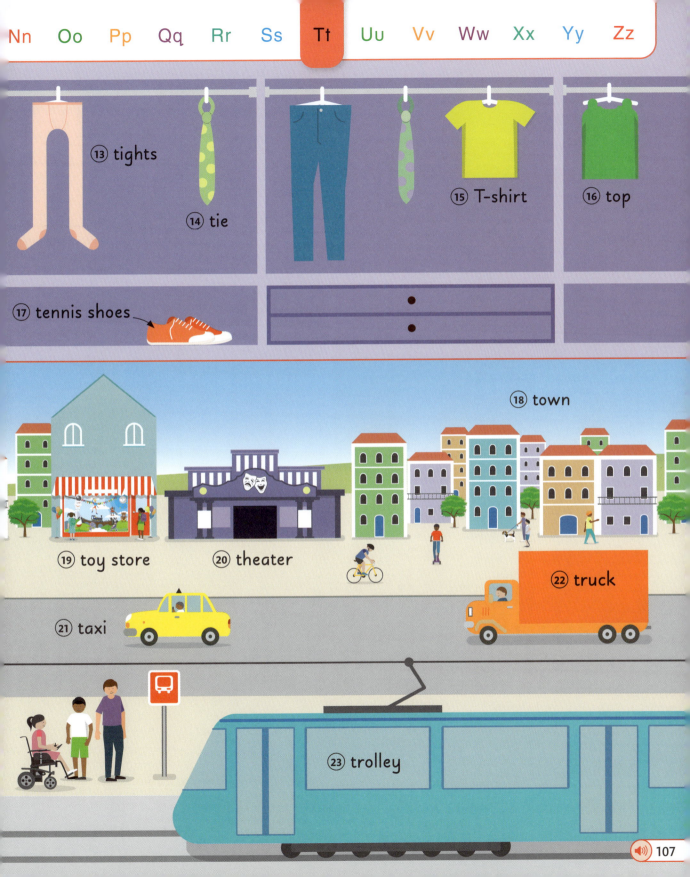

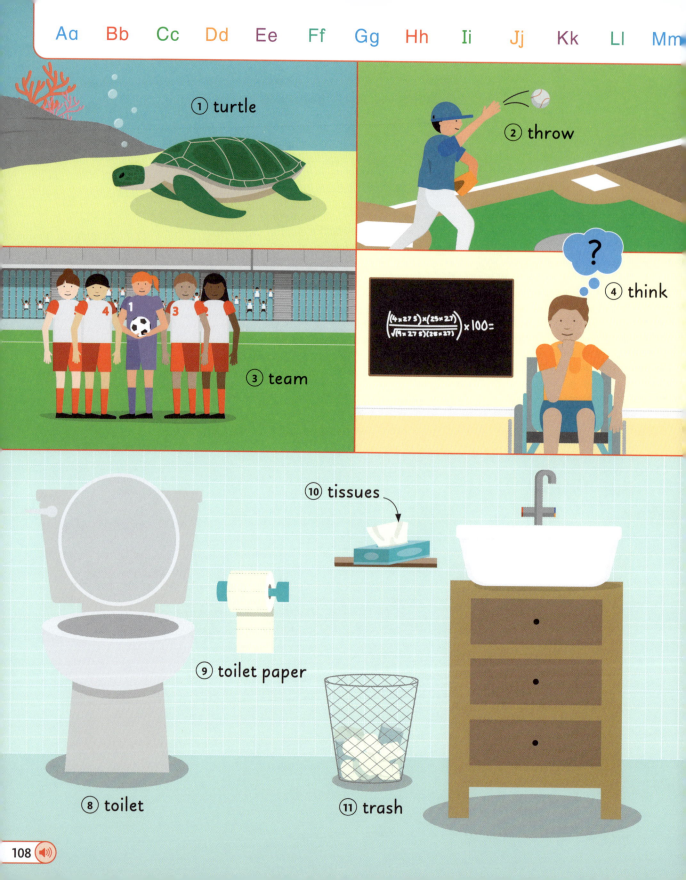

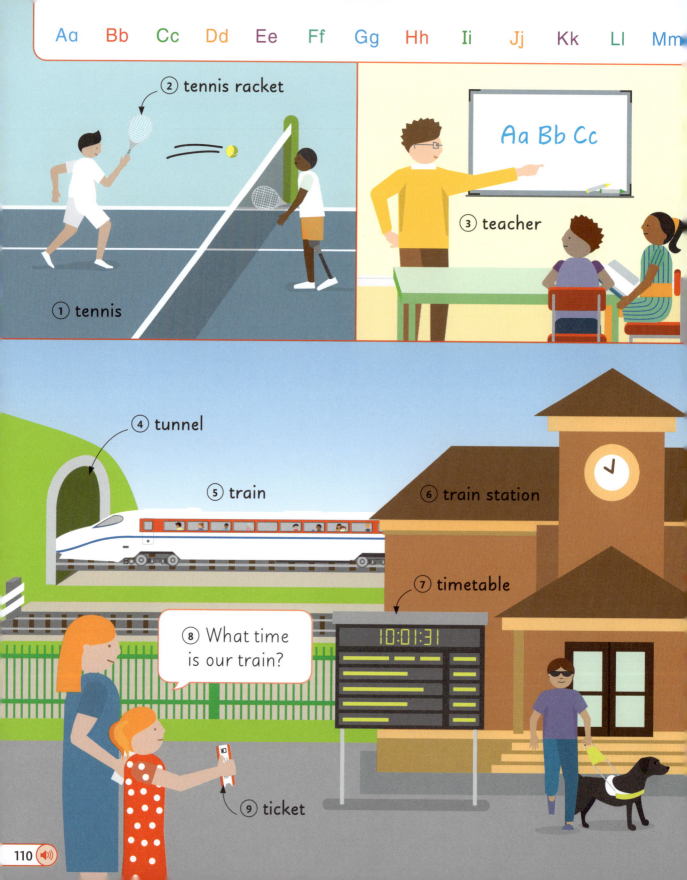

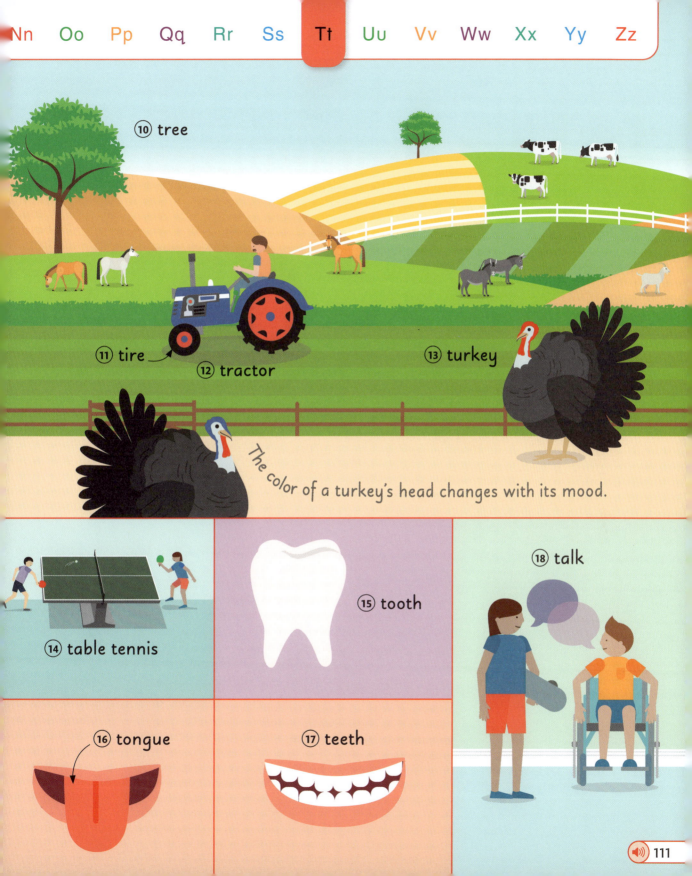

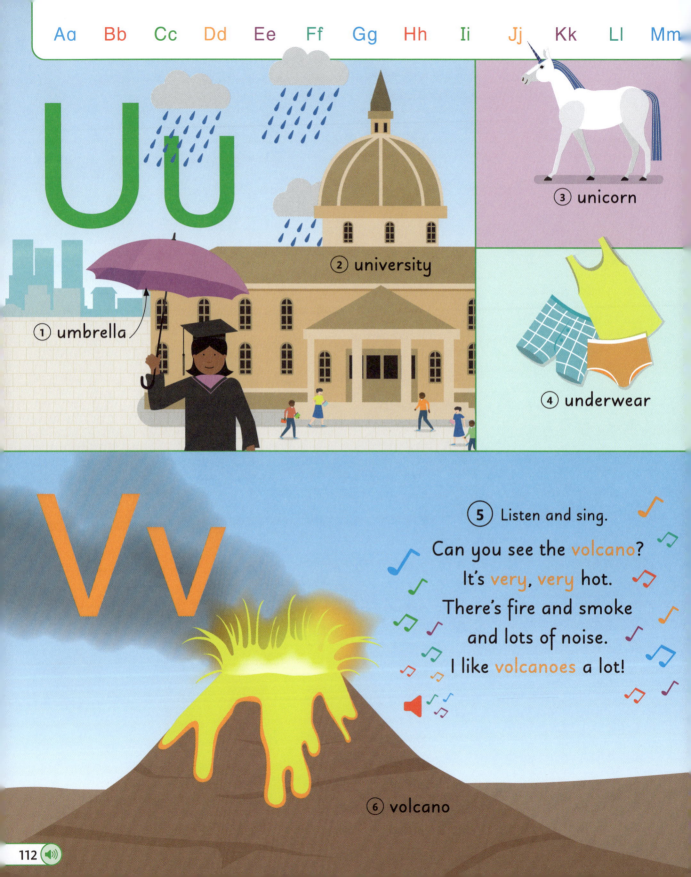

# Numbers

**0** ① zero  **10** ② ten  **20** ③ twenty  **30** ④ thirty  **40** ⑤ forty  **50** ⑥ fifty

**60** ⑦ sixty  **70** ⑧ seventy  **80** ⑨ eighty  **90** ⑩ ninety

**91** ⑪ ninety-one  **92** ⑫ ninety-two  **93** ⑬ ninety-three

**94** ⑭ ninety-four  **95** ⑮ ninety-five  **96** ⑯ ninety-six

**97** ⑰ ninety-seven  **98** ⑱ ninety-eight  **99** ⑲ ninety-nine

**100** ⑳ one hundred  **1 000** ㉑ one thousand  **1 000 000** ㉒ one million

# In the classroom

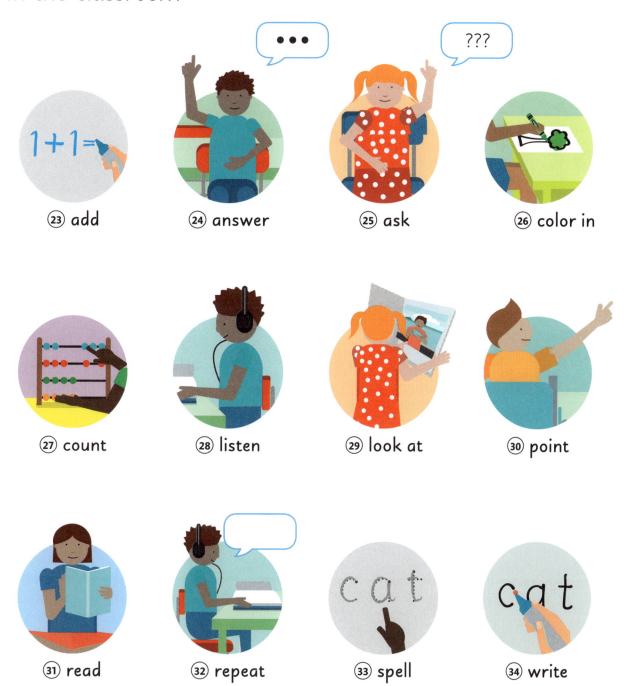

# Time

12:00 ② hour

12:01 ③ minute

12:01:51 ④ second

① clock

⑤ noon

⑥ midnight

⑦ day

⑧ week

⑨ weekend

⑩ month

⑪ year

⑫ What day is it?

## Prepositions

⑬ on

⑭ in

⑮ next to

⑯ behind

⑰ over

⑱ under

⑲ between

⑳ in front of

## Directions

㉑ left

㉒ right

㉓ up

㉔ down

## Positions

㉕ top

㉖ middle

㉗ bottom

# Useful phrases

# Feelings

125

# Opposites

 ① above
 ② below
 ③ young   ④ old

 ⑤ easy
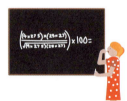 ⑥ difficult
 ⑦ light
 ⑧ heavy

 ⑨ stop
 ⑩ go
 ⑪ cheap
 ⑫ expensive

 ⑬ few
 ⑭ many
 ⑮ front
 ⑯ back

⑰ near  ⑱ far

⑲ inside  ⑳ outside

㉑ downstairs  ㉒ upstairs

㉓ like  ㉔ don't like

㉕ hot  ㉖ cold

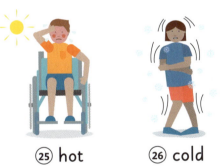

㉗ strong  ㉘ weak

㉙ high

㉚ low

# Opposites (continued)

# Word List

Each word is followed by the number of the page it appears on.

## KEY
| | |
|---|---|
| adj | adjective |
| n | noun |
| num | number |
| prep | preposition |
| pron | pronoun |
| v | verb |

## A
above *adj* 126
action figure *n* 12
actor *n* 13
add *v* 121
address *n* 12
adhesive bandage *n* 54
airplane *n* 10
airport *n* 10
alarm clock *n* 12
alligator *n* 12
alphabet *n* 12
ambulance *n* 11
anchor *n* 12
angry *adj* 125
animals *n* 13
ankle *n* 17
answer *v* 121
ant *n* 13
antelope *n* 13
apartment block *n* 10
apple *n* 10
apricot *n* 10
April *n* 67
apron *n* 10
archery *n* 13
arm *n* 17
armchair *n* 12
arrow *n* 13
art *n* 11
art *n* 100
artist *n* 11
ask *v* 121
asleep *adj* 12
astronaut *n* 12
audience *n* 13
August *n* 67
aunt *n* 43
avocado *n* 10
awake *adj* 12

## B
baby *n* 19
back *adj* 126
backpack *n* 18
bad *adj* 128
badger *n* 14
badminton *n* 16
baker *n* 23
bakery *n* 23
balcony *n* 22
ball *n* 16
balloon *n* 21
banana *n* 21
band *n* 21
bank *n* 22
bark *n* 15
barn *n* 15
baseball *n* 16
baseball cap *n* 16
basket *n* 22
basketball *n* 16
bat *n* 15
bat *n* 16
bathroom *n* 18
bathtub *n* 18
beach *n* 18
beach ball *n* 18
beads *n* 20
beak *n* 14
beans *n* 15
bear *n* 15
beard *n* 41
beaver *n* 14
bed *n* 19
bedroom *n* 19
bee *n* 14
beehive *n* 15
beetle *n* 14
behind *prep* 123
below *adj* 126
belt *n* 20
bench *n* 22
between *prep* 123
bicycle *n* 22
big *adj* 129
bird *n* 14
birthday party *n* 21
black *n* 28
blackberry *n* 14
blanket *n* 19
blinds *n* 19
blossom *n* 14
blue *n* 28
blueberries *n* 21
board game *n* 15
boat *n* 18, 23
body *n* 17
bone *n* 17
book *n* 19
bookcase *n* 19
bookstore *n* 22
boot *n* 20
bored *adj* 125
bottle *n* 18
bottom *adj* 123
bounce *v* 16
bow *n* 20
bowl *n* 21
bowling *n* 16
box *n* 20
boy *n* 79
bracelet *n* 20
branch *n* 15
bread *n* 21, 23
breakfast *n* 21
bricks *n* 20
bridge *n* 22
broccoli *n* 15
broom *n* 20
brother *n* 42
brown *n* 28
bubble *n* 18
bucket *n* 19
buckle *n* 20
build *v* 20
builder *n* 20
building *n* 20
bull *n* 14
burger *n* 21
bus *n* 20
bus station *n* 20
bus stop *n* 20
butter *n* 21
butterfly *n* 14
button *n* 20
buy *v* 23

## C
cabbage *n* 29
cabinet *n* 25
café *n* 33
cake *n* 30
calendar *n* 26
camel *n* 33
camera *n* 26
camp *v* 31
campfire *n* 31
can *n* 27
candle *n* 33
candy *n* 30
car *n* 33
card *n* 24
carnival *n* 25
carpet *n* 25
carrot *n* 29
carry *v* 29
cart *n* 27
cash register *n* 27
castle *n* 32
cat *n* 24
catch *v* 29
caterpillar *n* 32
cauliflower *n* 29
cave *n* 30
ceiling *n* 25
celery *n* 29
center *n* 32
cereal *n* 24
chain *n* 22
chair *n* 26
chalk *n* 27
cheap *adj* 126
cheese *n* 31
cheetah *n* 26
chef *n* 33
cherry *n* 30

chess n 26
chest n 17
chick n 32
chicken n 31
chicken n 32
children n 79
chin n 41
chocolate n 30
chopsticks n 33
circle n 102
circus n 25
city n 33
clap v 29
classroom n 27
claw n 24
clean adj 129
clean v 29
cliff n 30
climb v 30
clock n 26, 122
closed adj 128
clothes n 24
cloud n 33
cloudy adj 115
clown n 24
coat n 31
cobweb n 32
coconut n 24
coffee n 30
coin n 27
cold adj 127
cold n 55
collar n 24
college n 33
color v 27
color in v 121
colors n 28
comb n 24
comet n 31
comic book n 32
compass n 30
computer n 26
cone n 102
cook v 33
cookie n 30
coral n 31
corn n 29
corner n 32
cotton candy n 24

couch n 25
cough n 55
count v 27, 121
cousins n 43
cow n 32
crab n 31
crayon n 27
crocodile n 26
crown n 32
cry v 25
cube n 102
cucumber n 29
cup n 30
cupcake n 30
curly adj 52
curtain n 25
cushion n 25
customer n 30
cut v 27
cutlery n 27
cutting board n 29
cycle v 33

## D

dad n 42
dance v 34
dark adj 128
daughters n 42
day n 122
days of the week n 37
December n 67
deck chair n 35
deer n 34
dentist n 36
desert n 34
desk n 36
dessert n 35
diamond n 102
dictionary n 34
different adj 128
difficult adj 126
dining room n 36
dinner n 35
dinosaur n 36
dirty adj 129
dive v 35
diving board n 35
doctor n 36

dog n 34
doll n 36
dollhouse n 36
dolphin n 36
donkey n 34
don't like v 127
door n 36
down prep 123
downstairs n 127
dragon n 36
dragonfly n 34
draw v 36
drawer n 36
dream v 36
drill n 104
drink v 35
drinks n 35
drive v 34
drum n 36
dry adj 129
duck n 34
duckling n 34

## E

eagle n 38
ear n 39, 41
earache n 55
earring n 39
Earth n 39, 82
east n 30
easy adj 126
eat v 39
eel n 39
egg n 38
eggplant n 39
eight num 71
eighteen num 71
eighty num 120
elastic wrap n 54
elbow n 17
elephant n 38
eleven num 71
empty adj 128
English n 100
entrance n 39
envelope n 39
eraser n 39
excited adj 125

exit n 39
expensive adj 126
explorer n 38
eye n 39, 41
eyebrow n 39, 41
eyelash n 39

## F

face n 17, 41
fall n 97
family n 42
far adj 127
farm n 40
farmer n 40
fast adj 128
father n 42
February n 67
fence n 45
few adj 126
field n 40
fifteen num 71
fifty num 120
fin n 41
finger n 17, 51
fingernail n 51
finish v 45
fire n 40
fire engine n 40
fire station n 40
firefighter n 40
fireworks n 44
fish n 41
fishing rod n 45
five num 71
flag n 45
flamingo n 41
flashlight n 44
flippers n 41
floor n 44
flour n 44
flower n 40
fly n 45
fly v 41
foggy adj 115
food n 44
foot n 17
forest n 45
fork n 27

131

forty *num* 120
four *num* 71
fourteen *num* 71
fox *n* 45
Friday *n* 37
fridge *n* 44
fries *n* 44
frog *n* 45
front *adj* 126
fruit *n* 44
full *adj* 128

## G
garage *n* 47
garden *n* 46
garlic *n* 49
gate *n* 47
gazelle *n* 48
geography *n* 100
gift *n* 49
giraffe *n* 48
girl *n* 79
give *v* 49
glass *n* 49
glasses *n* 46
gloves *n* 46
glue *n* 49
go *v* 126
goal *n* 48
goat *n* 49
goggles *n* 48
goldfish *n* 49
golf *n* 49
good *adj* 128
goose *n* 49
gorilla *n* 48
granddaughter *n* 43
grandfather *n* 43
grandma *n* 42
grandmother *n* 42
grandpa *n* 43
grandparents *n* 43
grandson *n* 43
grapes *n* 46
grass *n* 47
grasshopper *n* 47
gray *n* 28
green *n* 28

greenhouse *n* 46
grow *v* 47
guitar *n* 48
gym *n* 49
gymnastics *n* 49

## H
hair *n* 52
hair dryer *n* 52
hairbrush *n* 52
hairdresser *n* 52
half *adj* 129
hall *n* 51
hammer *n* 104
hand *n* 17, 51
handlebar *n* 22
happy *adj* 125
hard *adj* 128
hat *n* 51
hay *n* 53
head *n* 17
headache *n* 55
headphones *n* 51
health *n* 54
hear *v* 90
heart *n* 102
heavy *adj* 126
hedgehog *n* 52
helicopter *n* 50
helmet *n* 51
hide *v* 53
high *adj* 127
hill *n* 53
hippo *n* 50
history *n* 100
hit *v* 53
honey *n* 50
hoof *n* 53
hook *n* 51
hop *v* 53
horse *n* 53
horse riding *n* 53
hospital *n* 50, 54
hot *adj* 127
hot-air balloon *n* 50
hotel *n* 50
hour *n* 122
house *n* 50

hug *v* 53
hummingbird *n* 52
hungry *adj* 125
husband *n* 43

## I
ice *n* 56
ice cream *n* 57
ice-cream truck *n* 57
ice hockey *n* 57
ice pop *n* 57
ice rink *n* 57
ice skate *n* 57
ice-skating *n* 57
iceberg *n* 56
igloo *n* 56
in *prep* 123
in front of *prep* 123
insects *n* 56
inside *adj* 127
instruments *n* 56
iron *n* 56
island *n* 57

## J
jacket *n* 59
jaguar *n* 58
jam *n* 59
January *n* 67
jar *n* 59
jeans *n* 59
jellyfish *n* 58
jewelry *n* 59
jigsaw puzzle *n* 58
jobs *n* 58
juice *n* 59
July *n* 67
jump *v* 58
June *n* 67
jungle *n* 58
Jupiter *n* 82

## K
kangaroo *n* 60
kettle *n* 61
key *n* 61

key ring *n* 61
keyboard *n* 26
kick *v* 61
king *n* 61
kitchen *n* 61
kite *n* 61
kitten *n* 61
kiwi *n* 61
knee *n* 17
knife *n* 27, 61
knit *v* 61
knuckle *n* 51
koala *n* 60

## L
ladder *n* 65
ladybug *n* 62
lake *n* 65
lamb *n* 65
land *n* 64
languages *n* 100
laptop *n* 63
laugh *v* 64
leaf *n* 62
left *adj* 123
leg *n* 17
lemon *n* 65
lemonade *n* 65
leopard *n* 62
letter *n* 63
letters *n* 63
lettuce *n* 65
librarian *n* 65
library *n* 65
life jacket *n* 64
lifeguard *n* 64
lift *v* 64
light *adj* 126
light *adj* 128
lighthouse *n* 64
lights *n* 63
like *v* 127
lime *n* 65
lion *n* 62
listen *v* 63, 121
living room *n* 63
lizard *n* 62
llama *n* 65

lobster *n* 64
lollipop *n* 65
long *adj* 52
look at *v* 121
loud *adj* 129
low *adj* 127

# M

machine *n* 67
magazine *n* 69
magician *n* 66
mail carrier *n* 66
mailbox *n* 66
man *n* 79
mango *n* 68
many *adj* 126
map *n* 66
March *n* 67
market *n* 68
Mars *n* 82
mask *n* 54
mat *n* 67
match *n* 66
math *n* 100
May *n* 67
me *pron* 42
meal *n* 69
meat *n* 68
mechanic *n* 67
medicine *n* 54
meerkat *n* 69
melon *n* 68
men *n* 79
menu *n* 69
Mercury *n* 82
metal *n* 67
middle *adj* 123
midnight *n* 122
milk *n* 69
milkshake *n* 69
minute *n* 122
mirror *n* 66
mole *n* 66
mom *n* 42
Monday *n* 37
money *n* 69
monkey *n* 69
monster *n* 66

month *n* 122
months of the year *n* 67
moon *n* 68
mother *n* 42
motorcycle *n* 67
mountain *n* 69
mouse *n* 26
mouse *n* 66
mouth *n* 41
movie *n* 68
movie theater *n* 66
mud *n* 66
mug *n* 69
museum *n* 66
mushroom *n* 68
music *n* 68
musician *n* 68
mustache *n* 41

# N

nail *n* 104
nauseated *adj* 55
near *adj* 127
neck *n* 70
necklace *n* 70
Neptune *n* 82
nest *n* 70
new *adj* 128
newspaper *n* 70
next to *prep* 123
night *n* 70
nine *num* 71
nineteen *num* 71
ninety *num* 120
ninety-eight *num* 120
ninety-five *num* 120
ninety-four *num* 120
ninety-nine *num* 120
ninety-one *num* 120
ninety-seven *num* 120
ninety-six *num* 120
ninety-three *num* 120
ninety-two *num* 120
noon *n* 122
north *n* 30
nose *n* 41, 70
nostril *n* 70
notebook *n* 70

November *n* 67
numbers *n* 71
nurse *n* 70
nuts *n* 70

# O

oar *n* 72
ocean *n* 72
October *n* 67
octopus *n* 72
off *adj* 73
office *n* 73
old *adj* 126
old *adj* 128
olive *n* 72
on *adj* 73
on *prep* 123
one *num* 71
one hundred *num* 120
one million *num* 120
one thousand *num* 120
onion *n* 72
open *adj* 128
orange *n* 28
orange *n* 72
ostrich *n* 73
otter *n* 73
outside *prep* 127
oval *n* 102
oven *n* 72
over *prep* 123
owl *n* 73

# P

package *n* 75
paint *n* 78
paint *v* 76
paintbrush *n* 76
painting *n* 76
pajamas *n* 77
palace *n* 82
palm *n* 51
pancakes *n* 81
panda *n* 78
pants *n* 81
paper *n* 78
paper clip *n* 80

parents *n* 42
park *n* 80
parking garage *n* 75
parrot *n* 79
party *n* 78
passenger *n* 79
pasta *n* 77
patch *n* 79
path *n* 80
patient *n* 54
pattern *n* 77
paw *n* 81
pea *n* 74
peach *n* 74
peacock *n* 82
pear *n* 74
pedal *n* 22
pen *n* 78
pencil *n* 78
pencil case *n* 78
penguin *n* 74
people *n* 79
pepper *n* 74
pepper *n* 77
perfume *n* 78
pets *n* 81
phone *n* 76
photo *n* 76
piano *n* 76
picnic *n* 80
pie *n* 80
pig *n* 75
pillow *n* 76
pilot *n* 79
pineapple *n* 74
pink *n* 28
pirate *n* 79
pizza *n* 77
plain *n* 77
plane *n* 79
planets *n* 82
planner *n* 78
plant *n* 76
plastic *n* 80
plate *n* 77
play *v* 76
playground *n* 81
plum *n* 74

133

pocket n 77
point v 121
polar bear n 74
police car n 75
police officer n 75
police station n 75
pond n 80
pony n 75
popcorn n 80
post office n 75
postcard n 81
poster n 76
pot n 76
potato n 74
present n 78
prince n 82
princess n 82
printer n 76
puddle n 80
pull v 75
pumpkin n 74
puppet n 76
puppy n 81
purple n 28
purse n 81
push v 75
pyramid n 81

Q
queen n 83
quiet adj 129

R
rabbit n 84
raccoon n 84
race n 84
race car n 87
radio n 85
railroad track n 85
rain n 86
rainbow n 86
raincoat n 86
rainforest n 87
rainy v 115
raisins n 86
raspberries n 86
read v 87, 121

rectangle n 102
recycle v 86
red n 28
reindeer n 84
relaxed adj 125
remote control n 85
repeat v 121
restaurant n 86
rhinoceros n 87
ribbon n 84
rice n 86
right adj 123
ring n 86
river n 84
road n 85
robot n 87
rock n 84
rocket n 87
rocking horse n 87
roller coaster n 85
roller skates n 87
roof n 85
room n 85
rope n 84
rug n 85
ruler n 84
run v 84

S
sad adj 125
sail n 93
sailboat n 93
salad n 97
salt n 89
same adj 128
sand n 90
sandals n 103
sandbox n 94
sandcastle n 94
sandwich n 97
Saturday n 37
Saturn n 82, 88
sauce n 91
sausage n 91
scales n 90
scarecrow n 101
scared adj 125
scarf n 88

school n 98
science n 100
scissors n 89
scooter n 94
score n 98
score v 102
screen n 26
screw n 104
screwdriver n 104
scuba diver n 92
sea n 92
seagull n 93
seahorse n 93
seal n 90
seasons n 97
seat n 22
seat n 95
seatbelt n 95
seaweed n 92
second n 122
see v 90
seeds n 101
seesaw n 94
sell v 101
semi-circle n 102
senses n 90
September n 67
seven num 71
seventeen num 71
seventy num 120
sew v 89
shampoo n 99
shapes n 102
shark n 93
shed n 100
sheep n 96
shelf n 99
shell n 92
ship n 92
shirt n 103
shoelace n 103
shoes n 103
shopping center n 99
short adj 52
short adj 129
shorts n 103
shoulder n 17
shout v 101
shovel n 94

shower n 99
shy adj 125
sick adj 55
sidewalk n 99
sing v 95
singer n 95
sink n 99
sister n 42
sit down v 98
six num 71
sixteen num 71
sixty num 120
skate v 101
skateboard n 94
skeleton n 17
ski v 88
skirt n 103
skull n 17
sky n 101
skyscraper n 98
sled v 88
sleep v 91
sleeping bag n 91
sleeve n 103
slide n 94
slippers n 103
slow adj 128
slug n 100
small adj 129
smell v 90
smile n 95
smoke n 90
snail n 101
snake n 96
sneakers n 103
sneeze n 55
snow n 89
snowball n 89
snowboard n 88
snowflake n 89
snowman n 88
snowy v 115
soap n 99
soccer n 98
socks n 103
soft adj 128
son n 42
song n 95
sore adj 55

134

soup n 97
south n 30
space n 88
spaceship n 88
spade n 100
spaghetti n 91
spell v 102, 121
sphere n 102
spices n 89
spider n 101
spinach n 97
spoon n 27, 97
sports n 102
spring n 97
square n 102
squirrel n 96
stable n 96
stadium n 98
stage n 95
stairs n 103
stamp n 96
stand up v 98
stapler n 96
star n 102
starfish n 92
stars n 88
step n 103
stick n 101
stingray n 93
stomach n 17
stomachache n 55
stone n 100
stop v 126
store n 98
storm n 95
stormy adj 115
story n 96
straight adj 52
strawberry n 100
stream n 96
street n 98
stretch v 101
stretcher n 54
strong adj 127
student n 101
study v 101
subjects n 100
submarine n 92
sugar n 89

suitcase n 90
summer n 97
sun n 82, 88
sun hat n 90
Sunday n 37
sunglasses n 90
sunny adj 115
surf v 92
surfboard n 92
surprised adj 125
swan n 96
sweater n 88
swim v 91
swimming pool n 91
swimsuit n 91
swing n 94
syrup n 89

## T

table n 105
table tennis n 111
tablecloth n 105
tablet n 106
tadpole n 104
tail n 105
talk v 111
tall adj 129
tambourine n 109
tape measure n 104
taste v 90
taxi n 107
tea n 105
teacher n 110
team n 108
teapot n 105
teddy bear n 106
teeth n 111
telescope n 105
television n 106
ten num 71, 120
tennis n 110
tennis racket n 110
tennis shoes n 107
tent n 105
theater n 107
thermometer n 54
think v 108
thirsty adj 125

thirteen num 71
thirty num 120
three num 71
throw v 108
thumb n 51
Thursday n 37
ticket n 110
tie n 107
tiger n 105
tights n 107
timetable n 110
tire n 22, 111
tissues n 108
toad n 104
toast n 105
toaster n 105
toe n 17
toilet n 108
toilet paper n 108
tomato n 106
tongue n 111
toolbox n 104
tools n 104
tooth n 111
top adj 123
top n 107
tortoise n 104
touch v 90
towel n 109
town n 107
toy box n 106
toy store n 107
toys n 106
tractor n 111
traffic n 106
traffic lights n 106
trailer n 105
train n 110
train set n 106
train station n 110
trash n 108
treasure n 106
tree n 111
triangle n 102
triangle n 109
tricycle n 106
trolley n 107
truck n 107
trumpet n 109

T-shirt n 107
Tuesday n 37
tunnel n 110
turkey n 111
turtle n 108
twelve num 71
twenty num 71, 120
two num 71

## U

umbrella n 112
uncle n 43
under prep 123
underwear n 112
unicorn n 112
university n 112
up prep 123
upstairs n 127
Uranus n 82

## V

van n 113
vase n 113
vegetables n 113
Venus n 82
vet n 113
video game n 113
view n 113
village n 113
violin n 113
volcano n 112
volleyball n 113

## W

waiter n 115
walk v 117
wall n 116
wallet n 115
walrus n 116
wash v 117
washing machine n 115
wasp n 114
watch n 115
watch v 117
water n 115
water v 114

waterfall n 117
watering can n 114
watermelon n 114
wave n 116
wave v 117
weak adj 127
weather n 115
website n 116
Wednesday n 37
week n 122
weekend n 122
west n 30
wet adj 129
whale n 116
wheel n 22, 115
wheelbarrow n 114
wheelchair n 115

whiskers n 116
whisper v 114
whistle v 114
white n 28
whole adj 129
wife n 43
windmill n 116
window n 116
windy adj 115
wing n 117
winter n 97
wolf n 117
woman n 79
women n 79
wood n 116
woodpecker n 117

woods n 117
wool n 116
worm n 114
worried adj 125
wrench n 104
write v 114, 121

## X
X-ray n 118
xylophone n 118

## Y
yacht n 118
yard n 118
yawn v 118

year n 122
yellow n 28
yoga n 118
yogurt n 118
young adj 126
yo-yo n 118

## Z
zebra n 119
zero num 120
zigzag n 119
zipper n 119
zoo n 119

# Acknowledgments

The publisher would like to thank:

Tim Woolf for songwriting; Kelly Adams, Adam Brackenbury, Anthony Limerick, and Anna Scully for design and illustration assistance; Ankita Awasthi Tröger, Elizabeth Blakemore, Thomas Booth, Amelia Petersen, and Carine Tracanelli for editorial assistance; Megan Douglass and Kayla Dugger for Americanization; Elizabeth Blakemore for proofreading; and ID Audio for audio recording and production.

All images are copyright DK. For more information, please visit www.dkimages.com.

# WHAT WILL YOU LEARN NEXT?

## BOOKS

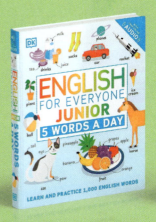

## FLASH CARDS